BO DON'T KNOW ME

MY YEAR WITH THE
1982-83 AUBURN TIGERS
A SHORT STORY
BY
FRED RILEY, JR.

FOREWORD

So, you think you want to be a college football coach? Then let's take a wild ride together through the 1982 Auburn football season with my good friend Fred Riley. I first met Fred in August 1982 when he joined the Auburn University football coaching staff as a graduate assistant. He was instrumental in helping me develop a special relationship with Coach Jack Crowe. Fred played quarterback for Coach Crowe at the University of North Alabama the two years prior to them both coming to Auburn. Coach Crowe was a tough and demanding coach, both physically and mentally. He expected his quarterbacks to exhibit mental toughness and preparedness, game management, great decision- making ability, limit turnovers, and the ability to execute our offense in intense situations. I remember several days after tough practice sessions where Fred helped me navigate the turbulence and stay focused on our team goals. Fred made me be a better quarterback!

Being a graduate assistant is a brutal and thankless job. But it's the best avenue to break into college coaching. In *Bo Don't Know Me*, Fred shares some interesting insights into the '82 season, along with some funny stories of the coaches and their locker room shenanigans and practical jokes. You'll also get the inside scoop on how the Auburn staff prepared for the Iron Bowl. You'll hear Fred's perspective on Pat Dye, Bo Jackson, many of the Auburn assistant coaches of the day and his fellow GA's. But my favorites are the stories of Fred's childhood, his family and how he became an "Auburn Man." I hope you enjoy this book as much as I did. It's great...to be...an Auburn Tiger! War Eagle!

Randy Campbell
82' AU QB

ISBN 979-8-9872693-1-2

Cover Design & Layout: Virginia Mathers

Back Porch Publishing, LLC
10681 Grace Lake Drive
Fairhope, AL 36532

Printed in the United States of America

In August 1982, I packed my 1978 Pontiac Firebird with all my personal belongings and began the drive from The University of North Alabama to Auburn University. I was pulled over for speeding on Highway 280, just outside Auburn. I explained to the officer my most important mission and hoped for forgiveness. He handed me a speeding ticket, smiled, and proclaimed, "Roll Tide!" I had been officially welcomed to the most intense rivalry in all of sports before reaching my destination.

I had grown up an Alabama fan and cried when they lost, which was not very often. That day, for the first time, I got to see life through the eyes of an Auburn fan. It would not be my last. I hope you enjoy this story of my personal transformation to becoming an Auburn Tiger. War Eagle!

DAY ONE

Coach Jack Crowe had been named offensive coordinator at Auburn under second-year Head Coach Pat Dye. Coach Crowe was my position coach at UNA, where I played quarterback in 1980 and 1981. We won the first conference championship in school history, and Coach Crowe and I had developed a strong personal relationship. Coach was a volatile man who … let's just say, coached us hard.

The main reason I played was that I could sort through the tone and process the information he was trying to get across. The other two guys struggled with his style. So, I went to Auburn at his request to work with him and help the quarterbacks in the passing game. I felt I could help the guys there process the information, and I assumed that was part of Coach Crowe's reasoning for asking me to come.

When I arrived at the athletic facility, I was immediately intimidated by the scale and intensity of everyone involved. I was not in Division II anymore. I found Coach Crowe's office and told him of my traveling incident, to which he replied, "We can get that handled." I was then introduced to Coach Dye.

Pat Dye was an intense man with an excellent feel for reading people, and it was evident he was getting a very quick read on me. After our introduction, I met the rest of the offensive coaching staff. I had a file cabinet in Coach Crowe's office that he shared with running back coach Bud Casey. Bud was a big man with a raspy voice from years of smoking. He shook my hand and welcomed me with a strong "nice to meet you, GA" (graduate assistant). Next, I met Coach Neil Callaway, who was very friendly but intense, like everyone there. He had played for Coach Bryant at Alabama but seemed friendly enough. (Interestingly, I coached his son Clay at Central Tuscaloosa in 1999.) He shared an office with Coach James Daniel. Coach Daniel was the most laidback of the group and offered a warm smile and handshake. The next member of the Offensive staff to meet was Wayne Bolt. Wayne was in a part-time type of position coaching the tight ends. He had played for Coach Dye at East Carolina and was a big man too with a quick laugh. Last, I saw Coach Larry Blakeney. Coach Blakeney had been at Vestavia High when I was a player at Minor in Birmingham. I had played a good game against his team, and he had come to our locker room to congratulate me, so I knew he was a good guy. Nothing happened during my time on the Plains to change my opinion of him.

The day was flying by, and it was time to get to Sewell Hall for dinner and figure out where I would be sleeping (since I had no idea). I had trusted Coach Crowe with my life and just figured he had everything under control. Once at Sewell, I went through the serving line and was invited by Coach Dye and Crowe to sit with them for dinner. I did not speak unless spoken to, and the first thing out of Coach Dye's mouth was, "Jack, our GA needs to get a haircut." I cringed on the inside, as I had just gotten a haircut the previous day and thought it to be a bit too short as it was. Oh well, I would be at the barber the next day and get a "real man's haircut" for the first time since I was a kid.

After dinner, I was introduced to Rusty and Sally Deen, the house parents of Sewell Hall and a lovely couple with strong Auburn ties. They settled me in and introduced me to my roommate, James Owens. Yes, James Owens—the first Black football player in Auburn football history. James was coming back to school to finish his degree. I had been at Auburn less than a day, and it had already been an amazing adventure. As it turned out, this was literally and figuratively just the beginning. War Eagle!

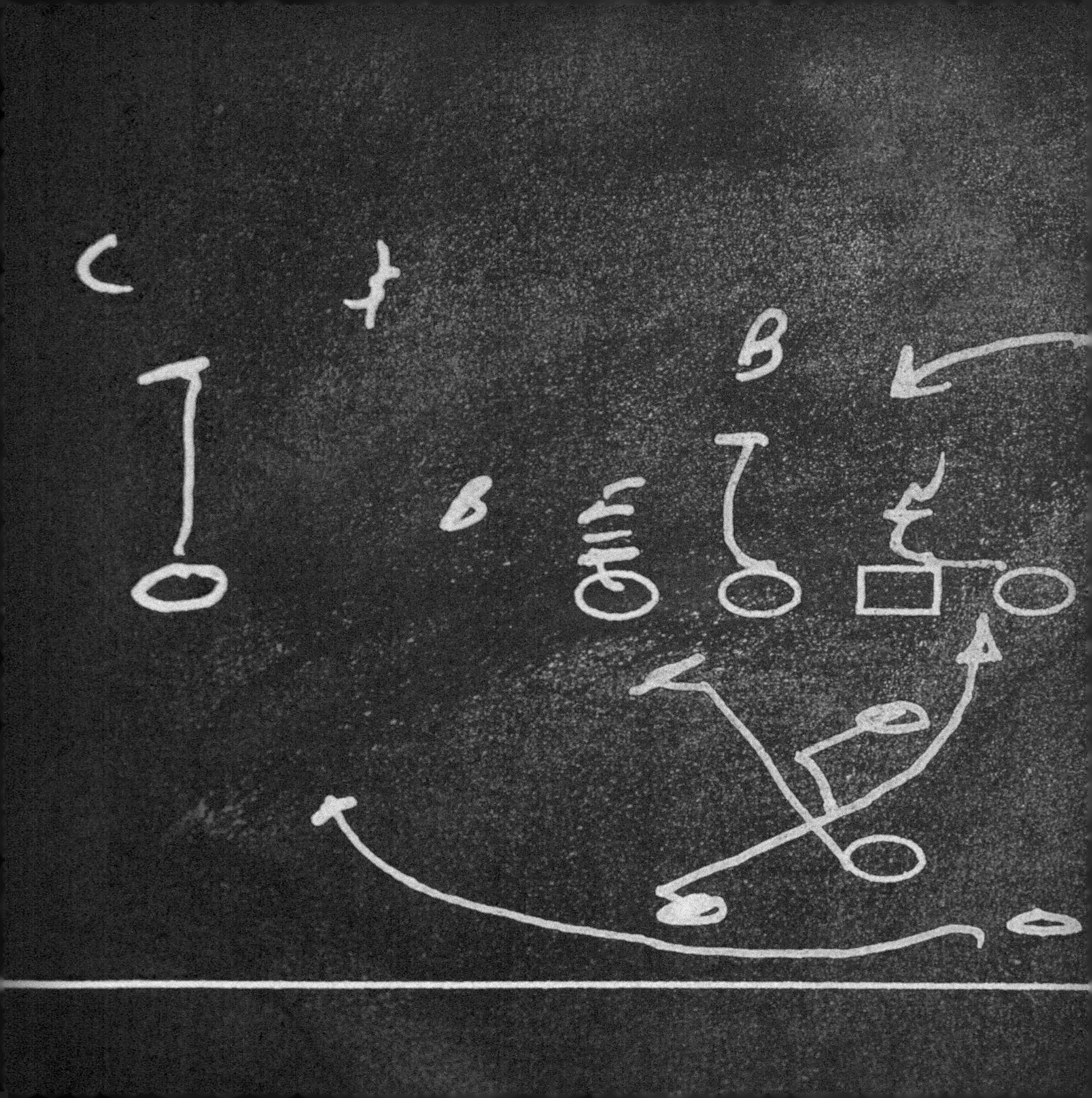
C
B
B

STAFF MEETINGS
AND A NEW UNIFORM

The staff met regularly early each morning. Days ran from 5 a.m. until after 10 p.m. most nights, and I had gone from a world of being a player and team captain to being a GA. This term was not a term of endearment by any means. It meant lowest of the low—do whatever you were told and do not speak unless spoken to. I was given a locker in the staff locker room and had a seat at the staff table; otherwise, my job was to make their jobs easier. Make coffee, go on Hardee's biscuit runs, take their dealer cars to get them serviced, fill their coffee cups—you name it.

Around the third day of meetings, Coach Dye points at me and states in his deep Southern drawl, "That one down there scares the hell outta me!" I had no idea how I could scare Pat Dye, but I sat in silence as it became clear I was an extra on the staff. You see, the NCAA rules at that time allowed for one volunteer/part-time coach, and Wayne Bolt filled that position, but there were an unlimited number of student assistants—James Owens, along with David Dorsey, Chip Creel, and a guy who would later become a dear friend, Marty Jackson. And there was just one more graduate assistant—Tim Stowers, who later became the head coach at Georgia Southern. So, technically, there was no spot for me (I later learned I was listed as a player that had not reported on the Sewell Hall dorm roster).

So, they were trying to figure out what to do with Riley. It was brought up that the NCAA allowed one official at practices to monitor/work with the schools on rules and whatnot. A call was placed to Frank Cox in the equipment room, and when I arrived at my locker for our first practice in shorts that fall, my Auburn gear was gone and replaced by an officials' jersey. This technically made me legal, as I spotted the ball during certain drills while doing my on-the-field work with the QBs dressed as an official. I hated that jersey, but I wanted to coach so badly that I would have worn an Aubie costume if necessary.

It had also become obvious that Coach Crowe had not really made any arrangements for me to be there. He just had me show up and hoped for the best. I occasionally heard the players comment on why I was wearing an officials' jersey, and some obviously thought I was a flake, but I had to keep things under wraps, as I was afraid that I could be removed from my position, as small as it was, at any time.

Practice in shorts had begun, and I enjoyed working primarily with Coach Blakeney and the QBs in the passing game. Randy Campbell was the starter, and we were roughly the same age, as he had been previously red-shirted. There was Clayton Beauford, who would later be moved to wideout; Mike Mann, a guy they called Superman because of his resemblance to Christopher Reeve; Pat Washington, a freshman from Murphy High in Mobile; and Gordon Stone, a walk-on from a place I had never heard of called Pine Apple, Alabama. I would offer to stay after practice and work with these guys individually, and all of them, at different times, took me up on it, so I did feel like I was helping a little. Campbell was great, as he had figured out my uniform dilemma and had quietly explained it to the team. On the other hand, the defensive staff hated my guts. Coach Crowe had given me way too much authority in their eyes, and they constantly knocked me down a peg or two whenever possible. Wayne Hall was the worst. He was a big tough man and a great player for Coach Bryant at Alabama. He gave me any possible duty he could and never used my name.

One funny moment was a practical joke instigated by Coach Hall in the staff locker room. I had returned from the shower and my chair was missing, and Coach Hall pointed to an empty chair and invited me to sit there. It was the first time he had acknowledged me as a human being, so I smiled, thanked him, and took the seat.

As I sat there drying off, a pair of feet appeared in my vision, and I looked up to find Coach Dye standing in front of me, naked with his privates right in my face asking me to "get the hell outta his chair." The room erupted in laughter, and I chose to not sit in the locker room anymore during my time on the Plains.

The rest of the defensive staff—Frank Orgel, Joe Whitt, and Bobby Wallace—had little or no use for me, though Coaches Hall and Wallace were the worst. I just kept getting them their coffee and biscuits and stayed away from them as much as possible. I later learned they treated most all GAs the same way over the years, and it was not personal; it was just their way. Oh, well. Welcome to the team. War Eagle!

FIRST DAY IN PADS
AND BO'S FIRST CARRY

Football practice at Auburn—and across the country—in 1982 was a matter of survival for most players. It was tough, it was bloody, and, if you were a walk-on, it was dangerous. Those poor guys were just sacrificial lambs to the football gods, and you would just move the drill if one went down.

Practice in pads was an unbelievable experience. Coach Dye later wrote a book called "In the Arena," and I am telling you, the practice field was like an arena on full-pad days. It was a sight to behold with Coach Casey screaming "blood on the saddle" and the defensive coaches destroying the walk-ons in their group. Offensively, our half-line periods were not for the faint of heart, as we blocked scout team players full speed and cut their knees with a maniacal passion. But the most intimidating picture was Coach Dye in that tower. Holy cow! He watched practice from that tower and did not miss a thing. He would not hesitate to call you out and no one wanted to be the subject of his wrath.

Coach Dye believed most passionately that the heart and soul of a team was established on the goal line. So, we finished the early practices with live goal line scrimmages. That first day we went to the 10-yard line going in with the first team defense (who had eight guys on that group end up in the NFL) ready to defend the endzone with their lives against the second team offense. The drill was set up to have a physically challenging ending to practice but also establish a great defensive mindset. The second offense was a solid unit but no match for these guys. In my mind, they were all nameless and faceless individuals, including a freshman right halfback ready to get his first snaps in live college football. So, Coach Crowe stepped into the huddle and called the toss—Sweep to the left, Right 57, I believe was the call. The ball was tossed to the right, with the halfback running the sweep to his left. The following five minutes changed Auburn football forever. You see, the right halfback was a freshman named Vincent Bo Jackson. The offense did not block a soul, but Bo Jackson made two guys miss and ran over a third to score a touchdown. The field grew silent, and whispers of "Did you see that?" could be heard. Then, the word that Coach Dye was coming down from the tower spread quickly. I am a fast learner and figured it best to be busy doing something, anything to appear busy, hoping he was not coming out of that tower after me. So, I did just that.

Coach Dye made his way to the huddle and quietly instructed Coach Crowe to run the play again. So, we sent the second offense to the line to face a pissed-off defensive group with the knowledge that we were likely to run the same play. Coach Crowe called Right 57, and we tossed it to this freshman halfback named Bo again. The result was even more astounding, as he broke a couple of tackles and ran over multiple defenders to score again. Coach Dye immediately put his arm around Bo and made a battlefield promotion declaring him the starting right halfback. Bo Jackson was never ever hit at an Auburn practice again. This did not sit well with the offensive coaches. Still, Coach Dye was wise enough to understand what he had just witnessed—he was the only one with the wisdom to see a legend had just been born on the Plains. We all now know Bo. War Damn Eagle!

BODY ODOR, BEER
AND BLACK COFFEE

So, the season opened with Wake Forest and Southern Miss, and we were 2-0 with Tennessee coming to town. During this time, I picked up some new duties. The first was doing cut-ups. Now, cut-ups are taking each individual play from the 16-millimeter game film, cutting them out and splicing them together on separate rolls for the coaches to look at the next day. Sounds easy, right? It might have been if someone had explained to us how it worked. If Tim Stowers had not come in and given us a little guidance, the first two game cut-ups would have been "stolen," and we would have pled the Fifth. Marty Jackson and I had been attempting to accomplish this task for a couple of hours when Tim came by and saw our mess. We had plays taped on the wall and divided into groups. It was a nightmare. He left and brought us back some beer because he realized we would be there most of the night. You see, there are small clear frames between each play, and the trick is to cut the film in those blank frames. Then, you tape the clear frames of each play together and start your reel of plays. The question of how much tape was never addressed, and we also did not know these would be upside down and/or backward if not connected properly. Also, you had to figure out how to tape shiny on shiny or dull on dull since each side of the film is different.

We worked for hours and finished up around 2 a.m. We proudly put our first reel on to watch our masterpiece. The tape was so thick it just exploded the projector mechanism apart. So now we have to go back and check the tape thickness on each splice and make further adjustments. We tried again, and that was when we learned about the upside-down and backward curse. So, each clip that was upside down and/or backward had to be redone and reloaded. By this time, it was approaching 5 a.m., and Coach Dye and Coach Crowe were notorious for trying to beat the other to work in the mornings. As Coach Dye once said, "That redheaded bastard is the only SOB that has ever beat me to work." A little after 5 a.m., we have what we have of the cut-ups, and both coaches roll in soon after.

We have been there all night working on those films and drinking beer—no telling how bad we look and smell. Of course, the first thing they both wanted was to see the cut-ups. We asked them which plays they would like to see, and each coach picked their stack and went to film rooms to get their first look. It took around three minutes before Coach Dye came out screaming and cussing us. We both went in and took our ass chewing, and then he allowed us to explain what our evening had been like. He just sat there glaring at us and then burst out laughing as hard as I have ever seen a man laugh. He had obviously observed our noticeable lack of sleep and maybe the fact that we still had our same clothes on from the previous day and smelled of a mixture of beer, body odor, and black coffee. He told us to get some rest and come back by our 8 a.m. staff meeting and redo the cut-ups that night. I am proud to say the next batch was much better, and by the end of the season, Marty and I could knock out a game in an hour or so.

Another duty assigned by Coach Hall was to stay in his office all night on Sunday night and watch the printer spit out the computer report on the next opponent. He said since we were already doing cut-ups, we could just check on this periodically. He failed to mention that this process took most of the night; after our first round of cut-ups, we could be finished by 11 p.m. or so on Sundays. So, for two nights, I slept on his office floor, listening to the printer run and fixing paper jams. Fortunately, someone rescued me from this hell, as I was told later that I didn't need to continue pulling the all-nighter. My guess is Coach Dye figured out this abuse was going on and put an end to it. I can promise you Coach Hall would have had me do it all year without giving it a second thought, but that was the life of a GA. War Eagle!

39 Draw vs Tennessee

TOUCHDOWN AUBURN!

My role on game day was an interesting arrangement, to say the least. Because I was technically an official, I could not wear any Auburn gear. I was given a press box pass, and Coach Crowe had me charting linebacker patterns. This entailed having multiple blank formation sheets where I would draw the play, chart the movement of the linebackers during said play, and have these ready for Coach Crowe at halftime. I wore a headset with no mouthpiece where I could hear the play but could not be heard. (Remember, do not speak unless spoken to.) I am at the back of the box and doing my charts as far removed from the other coaches as possible. I could not go on the field during warmups or anything else. I had my seat and my charts. Wearing my white button-down and khakis, I did my job. The first two games were uneventful, as I did my work and gave the information to Coach Crowe for him to use as he pleased.

Those first two games had solid crowds, but this was different. The pre-game touch football game between the managers of both universities, and the crowd arrived earlier and had a different buzz to it. Attendance that day was around 20,000 people stronger than the first two weeks, going over 75,000, as I best recall. Early in the game, it became very noticeable that when we ran to our left, the Tennessee backside inside backer was not respecting anything and just flying to the football. Chart after chart confirmed this, and he was making tackle after tackle. So, around the fourth possession, I eased down and showed the charts to Coach Blakeney. He gave me a thumbs up, and I returned to my spot at the top of the box. Suddenly, over the phones, I hear Larry say, "Hey Jack, Fred says the backside linebacker is running like hell on 39 plays, and 39 draw might be a big play." I cringed through this entire sequence of events as I knew the abuse that was coming. I wanted no credit; I just wanted to win. I had figured Larry would just give the intel to Jack and leave me out of it. Immediately, the offensive staff went absolutely nuts. "Fred said? Tell Fred to shut the hell up and get me a brownie from the press box" was the nicest statement I heard. But the one thing Jack Crowe knew about me was that he could trust me, and I would have never given him any information that was not 100 percent accurate. So, the next series begins with first and ten, Auburn from its own 20-yard line. Coach Crowe calls "Left 39 Draw."

My heart is pounding out of my chest as we go to the line of scrimmage. Bo has gotten a ton of attention now from defenses, and he is the right halfback; we are faking a play to the left and using Bo as a decoy to basically hand the ball to a pretty good football player named Lionel James—Big Train and Little Train. So, Randy Campbell takes the snap, and we fake the 39 option and hand the ball on an inside reverse (or draw as we called it) to Lionel. The backside linebacker runs like hell, and Lionel is at the 30, the 40, the 50, the 40, the 30, the 20, the 10, the 5 ... TOUCHDOWN AUBURN! Jordan-Hare goes wild, and I need a change of underwear. After all the craziness of the moment, Coach Blakeney gave me a thumbs up from his seat below, and no other coach ever acknowledged my involvement in the play. At halftime, I took Coach Wayne Bolt his brownie from the press box. Final score: Auburn 24, Tennessee 14. War Eagle!

NEBRASKA WEEK
AND BAMA ESPIONAGE

Holy cow, we are undefeated and ranked No. 20 in the country, and No. 8 Nebraska is coming to town. Yes, the Tom Osborne-led Cornhuskers complete with Dave Remington, Turner Gill, and Mike Rozier—the team that still lines up in the I formation and runs the sweep, belly, the power, and the belly option and destroys you with play-action passes. They're the same Nebraska that still has their quarterback block on running plays, the Nebraska that lines up on defense and smothers you.

We are playing with a 205-pound center on offense and may have a couple of guys on offense that could start for these guys. We now have all the distractions of being ranked and the attention that comes with it. We were coaching a team that could be really good but was not there yet, which was a big challenge for the staff. We were just trying to get better each day and each rep and focusing on not getting caught up in the big picture. But this was the Big Red Machine. Auburn fans are going crazy, enjoying the attention and the buzz more than ever under a Pat Dye-coached Auburn.

Behind closed doors, the coaches know we are in trouble with this bunch, but the task is to keep grinding and, just maybe, if you don't tell the team just how good Nebraska is, ignorance could be bliss. So, we do what we do. The staff does their work, and we do our cut-ups, pour the coffee, make the biscuit runs, and do anything else we are directed to do. In the meantime, Alabama is playing Arkansas State this week at 7:30 p.m. at Legion Field, and we are kicking off early. The staff is discussing sending me to Birmingham post-game with a recording device to steal Alabama's signals. I would just find a place to sit inconspicuously and say, for instance, "Play 1, touch nose, wave left arm." We would then match the signals that corresponded with the play on film. Brilliant! I was going to have a full weekend ahead. Then on Friday, Coach Dye got spooked and met with Coach Crowe and me and said he had decided against the plan. He felt that since I was from Birmingham originally, there was just too big a risk of someone identifying me and turning us in. So, we scrapped the plan. Oh well, on to Nebraska!

So, Saturday arrives and so do the Huskers. My God, they are enormous! I have to observe from the press box, but the difference even in warmups is obvious. This is not Wake or USM or even Tennessee. As we got seated, an excited student assistant

David Dorsey screamed at the top of his lungs, "Let's bring these MFers on!"

And "bring it" they did. A 41-7 butt whoopin' that was worse than the score indicated. We were physically whipped in every way possible and got to see up close and personal just how far we had to go to play and compete with a team of this caliber. The good news was that we have Kentucky and Georgia Tech the next two weeks at home finishing up a six-game home stand before we travel the first time to Starkville to face Mississippi State. We actually have eight home games this year, with three on the road, and one of those is Alabama at Legion Field. The schedule sets us up for some success if we can regroup and bounce back. Coach Dye is a master motivator of men, and it will be a great learning experience watching him handle the staff and the team. If anyone can do this, it is him. War Eagle!

FOUR WEEKS OF ROAD TRIPS
AND RANDOM EVENTS

Fans can be so fickle. After losing to Nebraska, our crowds fell to 55,000 the next two weeks. Come on, man! Johnny Majors at Tennessee had famously said that a football fan is someone who screams at an 18-year-old for not being able to throw a pass to another 18-year-old 50 yards away and then cannot even find his car after the game—and he is absolutely right.

Coach Dye is able to rally the troops masterfully, along with the staff, and the focus within the program is outstanding. To heck with anyone outside of the program. Auburn always seems to play better with a chip on their shoulder anyway and constantly works best when having an underdog mentality. I don't know why, but that seems to be how it goes. I have become solid friends with James Owens, who always was an outstanding man. He has been through things I could not have imagined, even though we share a common poor socioeconomic upbringing. He is away from his family working on his degree, and we spend time in our room just talking about family, life experiences, and dreams. We find out that we both want to be college head coaches one day. We both want to impact the world through coaching, and he finally realized his dream when he became the head football coach at Miles College sometime later. (I really miss No. 43, and the world is a lesser place without him.)

The team is improving as we beat Kentucky and Georgia Tech, and Al Del Greco kicks six field goals for all our 18 points in that win. A side note: I see a gentleman give Al $300 for each kick made in the parking lot after the game, so $1,800 total, and it hits me again just how different Division I is—and also reminds me that I am basically broke. Remember, at this point, I am not getting paid; I have food and shelter but no money for anything else. My parents are still sending me $100 a month to help until I move out into the "real world" on my own, but that does not buy much in terms of clothes or anything else—let's just say my fashion at the time was certainly not magazine worthy. Interestingly enough, Frank Young, an associate athletic director, called me into his office around this time and asked me, "Fred, do you have any money to go out to eat or purchase clothes and whatnot?" I told him about the $100 my parents provided and that I didn't have much time for a social life anyway. He smiled, handed me $300, thanked me for my hard work, and told me not to mention the $300 to Coach Dye. This was the most money I had ever held in my hands at one time. I was genuinely speechless and never mentioned it to anyone—not James, Marty, or anyone else. I was just glad to get myself another shirt, some more khakis, and a pair of jeans. I was and have always been low maintenance, and this was a big deal for me.

So now we prepare for our first road game—Mississippi State in Starkville. I am unsure how I will get to the game since we have not traveled yet, and no one has given me any information. Late in the week, I asked Coach Crowe just how I would be getting to the game, and it really had not crossed his mind. Jack was always a very single-minded and focused individual, and I was not surprised. He decided the student assistants and I would drive a couple of vehicles to Starkville and stay in a room together. We needed to be at practice on Friday to handle our duties and would just pile into a room together that night. Remember, at that point, I am not allowed to show up on any list of any kind, as I am not officially working for Auburn. So, off we go together to Starkville. We stopped in Tuscaloosa at a shack called Dreamland BBQ, where I realize I had never really had good barbecue in my entire life until that day. Oh my God! It was a struggle to not get sauce all over me, but at least I now had a second pair of khakis if there was an accident.

We forged on to Starkville, handled our duties, and went to the hotel to check-in. It was there where I learned firsthand what a prima donna is. You see, six of us traveled together, and we had two rooms with three people in each room. Former kicker/punter Alan Bollinger was working as a student assistant with the kicking game. We did not see him around much, as he did not participate in all of the weekend and early morning or late night duties. So, our room was Alan, me, and Marty Jackson, and we were discussing who would get the single bed and who would sleep together. Alan then proclaims since he is the only true Auburn man in the room, he is declaring seniority and taking the bed. After much discussion, Marty and I decided we would rather sleep with one another than have to sleep with Alan anyway, so we let him have the bed. That was a win-win for all of us.

Game day arrives in Starkville. The press box is just awful. Even UNA had better facilities. It was hot, the windows would not open, and there were only four or five seats, so most folks were standing. Doing the charts is a chore standing up, and then, in the middle of the game, I kid you not—wasps begin falling out of nests from the ceiling. So now, the student assistants and I are killing wasps during an SEC football game, using our forms and papers to keep them off the coaches. Welcome to the big time! I don't remember much else about the game, but we win our first road game and are undefeated in the SEC.

Next up is Florida. They are led by Wilbur Marshall, and the Florida field will be a madhouse. We traveled to Gainesville in the equipment truck with the equipment managers. I completely underestimated what a hell of a situation this would be. There were about eight of us crammed in this vehicle. There was no air conditioning, and we were miserable even with the windows down. We were all soaked from sweat and smelled like goats when we arrived. We also had to go directly to the stadium to set up for practice and had no opportunity to shower or change clothes before the workout. The staff and team arrived, and our appearance must have been startling as Coach Crowe pulled me aside and told me I would be riding the bus for the rest of the trip and that I could sit beside him. I was thrilled and got to ride the team bus for the first time and did so for the rest of the trip. In my youthfulness, how this separated me from the other guys never crossed my mind. I was just happy to finally feel a little more of a part of the big picture. Looking back, I realize it was me who looked like the prima donna, but it just never occurred to me until many years later. I probably should have stayed on the equipment truck. We lost the next day on multiple controversial officiating calls, including a no-call when Wilbur Marshall hit Randy late and almost killed him, and an onside kick that was given to Florida late, and they kicked a game winning field goal as a result. We played so hard but came up two points short, as I recall. We now have three games left: two at home and Bama at Legion Field, so there do not appear to be any more equipment truck rides in my near future. War Eagle!

RUTGERS', RECRUITING LETTERS, AND THE SOUTH'S OLDEST RIVALRY

I truly do not remember the Rutgers game at all. Sorry. But what I do remember is that it was around that time of year when I was given the responsibility of working with the Tigerettes and writing all of Coach Crowe's recruiting letters for him. You see, each coach has girls assigned to them that recruit players from their recruiting area. My assignment was to meet with Coach Crowe's ladies and get insider information from them, as they have already been communicating with the recruits. I was then to write personal letters from Jack. A young lady named Pam was responsible for heading up Coach Crowe's group. She was from the Birmingham area and was very smart and savvy when it came to recruiting. There was a young recruit from Atlanta who had fallen in love with Pam, and she was the reason he was coming to Auburn. These kids were just so gullible, and these ladies knew how to handle themselves while keeping a professional distance. They were truly amazing. So, I wrote letter after letter, week after week, and Jack would sign them until I became good enough at it to forge his signature. You know the good Lord had not added any time to each day—this task was just added to my other duties. Fortunately, we had cutting film down to a science, and our routine was pretty streamlined now to the point I had time to get this done without much of a problem. So, we would meet, discuss each player, and talk about how their season was going, if they had won the previous week, and other needed topics. Using that discussion, I would put together something like this:

Dear Matthew,
Congrats on the big win last week! We are so proud of you and your performance! Good luck this week vs. City High, and remember, "The Eye of The Auburn Tiger is watching you!"
War Eagle!
Coach Jack Crowe

Pretty simple, huh? So, to you guys that are reading this and have letters from 1982 signed by Jack Crowe in a scrapbook somewhere—I am sorry, but they were from me.

Georgia week has arrived—truly, the South's oldest rivalry, and the Bulldogs had Herschel Walker and Vince Dooley. The expectations were that this would be a classic. We were working hard on our two-minute offense, and my job was to spot the ball in these drills. Remember now, I am supposed to be an official at practice. The offensive staff is having trouble with Bo and his route running, as they have expanded the offense, and Bo is also having trouble with his assignments. So, we rep it and rep it over and over, but we are still struggling. Wouldn't you know it—the Georgia game comes down to a two-minute drill. Lionel James has broken a great run and given us the lead in the fourth, but Georgia went back down the field and took the lead. We then have to execute our "Minute Man" offense, as we called it. We are on the move, and I silently listen on the headphones as Jack makes his calls and Randy drives us downfield. Still, when we get to the red zone, Bo has a couple of missed assignments, and things go sideways. Georgia stops us, and we lose 19-14.

The offensive staff is going crazy wearing Bo out on the phones. Coach Dye does not wear phones, so he does not hear all this. The Sunday morning staff meeting is more of the same. I sit quietly and listen to the moaning and groaning until finally, Coach Dye has had enough. "Listen to me and listen good. We wouldn't be in the position to have the season we are having without Bo Jackson. There's a bunch of folks, including folks in this room, we could have gotten here without, but he ain't one of them. So y'all shut the hell up, and I will coach Bo from now on. The sumbitch is going to win the Heisman one day, and some of y'all will be selling used cars." Or something to that effect. So, that discussion ended abruptly, and we headed into our open date before the Iron Bowl.

S   B   S

B   B

Bo. 1ST Run at

Practice "57"

OPEN DATES, WORKOUT DATES, AND A COUPLE OF BASKETBALL STORIES

Open dates allow for a little breathing room and time for self-evaluation. In addition to the fact that we traded all of our games with Bama for breakdown—which took us untold hours to dissect—and cut-ups are studied and recruits are courted, coaches find a little time to run or work out and maybe play a little lunchtime basketball. I learned when you were asked to join a coach for a workout or run, you said "Yes, sir," and went. No questions asked. Now, I hate running, I absolutely despise it, and if you see me running now, someone is probably chasing me. But now I am trapped by a few cross-country wannabe coaches who think this crap is fun. So, here we go running all over campus mile after mile, and I am dying, and I swear if I can get back to the arena, I will never do this again. I make it back and devise a plan for the next day to avoid this torture. I think I will sneak out and hide, I will lift weights—I will do anything but run again. The next day, Bud Casey says, "Hey, GA, to hell with that running. Come get a workout with me." Bud had a torn ACL and had not had it surgically repaired, so he had been dragging that leg around like the Walking Dead for months, and I knew this would be some slow-motion working out. I follow Bud to the locker room and change into my t-shirt and shorts. Bud drops his clothes in front of me, wraps a towel around himself, and tells me to follow him. So, being the good GA that I am, I follow Bud to the steam/sauna room in the basement of the facility, and Bud declares, "There is no workout like a good steam." I follow him into the sauna, where he drops his towel, sits naked, and smokes a cigarette while I sit in my shorts for 30 minutes, sweating my rear end off. Bud just talks and talks and smokes and smokes, while I nervously sweat and sweat. I never thought I would long for a cross-campus run, but there I was sitting with a naked, smoking, sweaty-ass man wishing I was anywhere else. Thankfully, that thirty minutes from hell ended, but then I had to devise a different lunchtime plan.

Now, Larry Blakeney, Bobby Wallace, and Wayne Bolt loved lunchtime basketball. Larry and Bobby were great athletes, and Wayne was a big body in the paint. I decided to join them and try my hand there. I mean, I was a college athlete, so surely I could hang with these guys. We were playing, and all was going well when a new women's basketball assistant asked if she could join us. The coaches said sure—we adjusted the teams, and since I was the youngest on the floor, I was assigned to cover the women's coach. This young woman was around six feet tall and had a very athletic build. We played our games to 10 by one point "Make 'em, Take 'em." With the coaches wearing me out, this young woman made ten straight baskets on me, winning the game 10-0. We never got the ball. With my head down in defeat and shame, she patted me on the rear and whispered, "It's okay, Coach—I was an All-American at NC State." I guess if you are going to get beat, it might as well be by an All-American.

One other basketball note is Charles Barkley was at Auburn at that time. Charles was a giant of a human being, and the staff had him on the salad bar cottage cheese diet plan, but he just kept gaining weight. So, they finally staked out the dorm after curfew, and, sure enough, thirty minutes after curfew, the pizza delivery car arrived with a few large pies for Charles along with a supply of beverages. The staff followed the delivery guy and then searched Charles' room to find stacks of empty pizza boxes and drink containers hidden in his closet and under his bed. My wife Susan was a student at Alabama and says that they would chant "Food World" at Charles when they played him. I wonder what they would have done with this bit of information.

Okay, moving on. Open Week is officially over now. Beat Bama!

THE 1982 IRON BOWL

Iron Bowl week has arrived, and it's time to focus on beating 'Bama. Here we go! The week begins ominously as Coach Hall decides to jump off the goal posts on the defensive practice field as the team yells, "Warrrr Eagle! Hey!" His plan is to land softly, hit the ground, and roll as the cheer hits its final note. It did not quite turn out the way it was planned. Coach Hall hit the ground, severely injured his ankle, and limped throughout the entire week. I must admit I laughed my rear end off privately and really had to fight laughing out loud at that moment. I am not so sure he didn't see me smile.

Looking back, it is still hard to believe I am in the middle of everything with all this swirling around me. As a child, I played my first game for the Graysville Firebirds at Legion Field. My father was an usher at Legion Field and was there when Snake Stabler ran his famous touchdown in the mud. My finest high school game at Minor was against Ensley at Legion Field during my senior year. It was a special place for me.

The rest of that week is a blur. The next thing I remember is the team being escorted by police to Legion Field with sirens blaring and the hair on my neck standing up (Yes, I got to ride the bus!).

We arrived at the stadium and went out to walk the field in street clothes, as was our routine. I had alerted my father to when we would be arriving and hoped he would be there to watch a little before they cleared the stadium of any potential spies. My dad was a very humble man and hated the spotlight. He would never want to intrude on anything, so I was pleasantly surprised to see him sitting in the stands by himself. I waved at him from a distance, and he smiled and waved back. I could see the pride and excitement on his face for his oldest son.

As I continued walking, Coach Dye called me over and asked if that was my daddy. I told him it was, and Coach did the most wonderful thing. He said, "Go get your daddy and tell him I would like to visit with him." I immediately ran over to the stands and told Dad about Coach Dye and his request, and at first, he declined. But after I explained that I would be in trouble if he told Coach no, Dad reluctantly eased down onto the field. For the next 15 minutes or so, I watched my dad, who was a lifelong Bama fan (but who was also rooting for his son), walk Legion Field with Pat Dye. I never asked what they talked about, and it did not really matter. It just showed what kind of man Coach Dye was and how observant he was of everything going on around him, even in the middle of preparation for this battle versus Coach Bryant.

My daddy became an Auburn fan that day, and I would forever be a Pat Dye fan.

That night, we returned to the hotel for our meal and meetings, and it was time for bed check and some fitful sleep. Marty and I had become good friends and actually got to room together for this trip. We were waiting for the elevator doors to open when we both heard his voice—Keith Jackson was on the elevator! We speak to Mr. Jackson briefly, welcome him to Birmingham, and ride the elevator up to our rooms, talking about our good fortune. This had been one unforgettable day, and we still had no idea what was in store for the following day!

Game Day. The Iron Bowl. Legion Field is filled with the traditional 50/50 crowd of orange and blue and crimson and white. Coach Bryant is leaning against the goalpost with his program rolled up in his hand. ABC is broadcasting the game with Keith Jackson and Bud Wilkinson. I have dreamed about this experience since I lived in the coal mining camps of Praco.

I settle into my seat at the top of the box, doing my charts and watching the linebackers. Bama is dominating the game, but they keep turning the ball over or have a drive-stopping penalty, and we keep hanging around. Coach Dye and the staff are focused when we reach halftime; we just need to get the game to the fourth quarter. That is where we will win, by playing hard for 60 minutes. We know this game will go to the last possession—so it does. Down 22-17, we begin our drive. We convert third downs and execute plays the best we have all day. We make it to the red zone and now the goal line. We are now at the 1-yard line. We have been practicing a particular play for a few weeks—43 over the top, which became "Bo over the top." Heck, he is the most outstanding athlete any of the coaches have ever seen. He could even be a high jump champion, as we would set up a pile of dummies and practice the play so he would have a soft place to land.

The stage was set, and the play call was no surprise: 43 over the top and...Touchdown Auburn! We go for two and miss the attempt, but now we just need to hold on and keep them from getting into field goal range. The defense plays its guts out, and victory is near. I leave my seat in the box and walk down to the front so I can get a better look at the end—to see the celebration and the handshake between Coach Dye and Coach Bryant up close. I looked at Coach Blakeney; he is sobbing, and I started crying because of him. You see, it had been a long time since we had beaten Bama, and, yes, you read that right—

I said "we." Until that day, I had just worked for Auburn. Now, I was an Auburn man. War Eagle!

The post-game celebration was insane. The SEC network has a story on the game and a video of us singing the fight song in the locker room. You can actually see me in the back. As far as I know, that is the only evidence that I was ever at Auburn, as I never took a picture. Coach Dye sent us back out to thank the Auburn fans for sticking with the team through thick and thin. Auburn folks love Auburn.

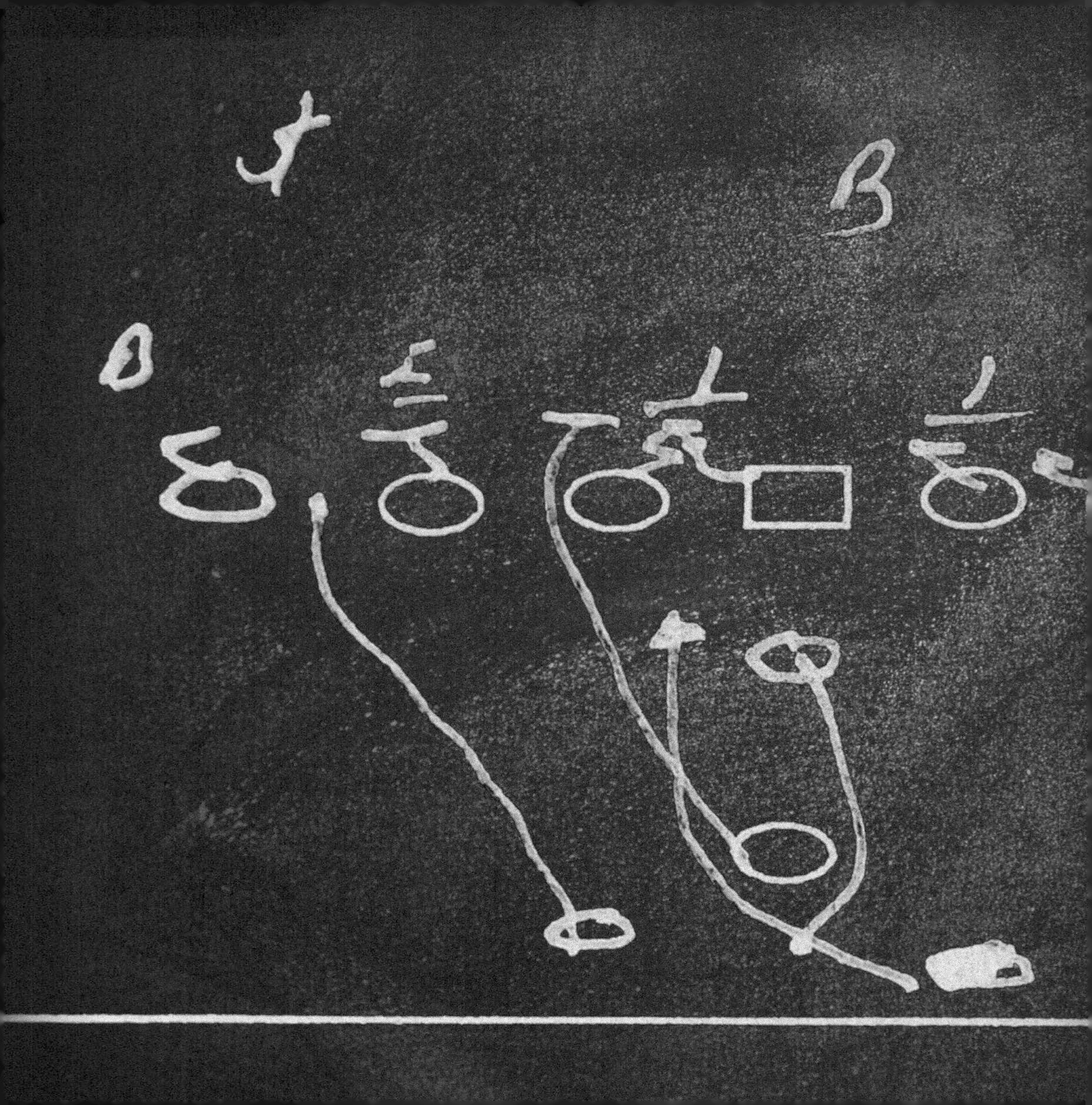
B

COAL MINING KID TO
MULTIPLE HEISMAN WINNERS

The 1982 football season ended an amazing journey to begin a coaching career. You see, I had been so blessed to have come so far in my 22 years. I had been brought home as a child in 1960 to the coal mining camp of Praco right outside of Birmingham. We did not have indoor toilets or heat until I was six years old. It was all outhouses and blankets. We then moved up to a coal-burning stove camp house and an indoor toilet. When I was eight, we had the finest house in the mining camp, with a window unit air conditioner and little gas heaters in each room. We had made it to the big time! It was around that time I was called to be a football coach. Yes, called, just like a preacher is called. I never wanted to be a policeman, fireman, or truck driver, and my father would have none of this coal mining stuff for his boys. My parents moved me and my younger brother Randy to Graysville because they saw education and athletics as our way out of the mines. They began putting money away each week for our college. We both received scholarships, so they used those monies to send us off into the world with cars—the 1978 Pontiac Firebird. So now, just 22 years removed, I was part of the Auburn Tigers' staff. For more perspective, when he was six years old, my dad was homeless, fatherless, and living in an abandoned railroad car.

He was 43 years old when I went to Auburn. He and Coach Dye were roughly the same age.

So, yes, I am a miracle, and this season was a miracle. I had a front-row seat to watch the greats like Bo Jackson, Mike Rozier, and Herschel Walker. And we were about to play Boston College and Doug Flutie in the Tangerine Bowl—four Heisman winners in one year along with the player the Remington Award is named after.

But, before I get too full of myself, let's get back to the bowl game. The team is flying to Orlando, so guess who cannot be on the passenger list? You got it. So, the staff devised a plan for me to drive a player's car to Orlando, Mark Dorminey, since he is from the Orlando area and will stay there for Christmas break. Then, post-game, I will fly back with the team as Mark. Great plan, right? As Theo Huxtable used to say, "No Problem!" So, we load up the car, and I begin the drive to Orlando with plans to meet the team at the hotel that night. Keep in mind that I have never driven to Orlando and am using an old-fashioned fold-up map from the glove box. I do not own a gas card, but I have what I assume is enough money for gas and food for the trip. So, in the early morning darkness, I depart Auburn for Orlando and work my way toward the hotel.

Somewhere in Florida, I encounter my first toll road. Now, I had never seen a toll road and did not even know there was such a thing. I quickly checked my finances and realized I may not have enough money to pay my last toll, and, sure enough, I was right. I arrive at the final toll booth just outside of Orlando, and I am broke. I do not have a dollar. So, I explained my dilemma to the toll booth operator and showed him my empty wallet. Somehow, someway, he let me pass. Thank you, Jesus! I arrived at the hotel in time for the team meeting, where I found, much to my surprise, that I was being included in the travel expenses for the trip and was given $800! This was almost triple the amount of money I had ever held in my hands, and I certainly never had that much money in any account of any kind in my life.

The week was outstanding, and I met all kinds of Red Sox fans who had made the trip. We won the bowl game, Auburn 33 – Boston College 26. Afterward, I was allowed to fly back with the team (my first plane ride) as Mark and visited with Coach Crowe about my coaching future and his thoughts for me. I was also informed that the NCAA was adjusting the limits on graduate assistants in January. I would officially be named a graduate assistant for the 1983 season and be able to start graduate school. No more officials' jerseys for me! War Eagle!

43 - Be over the Top

COACHING CLINICS, SPRING PRACTICE, AND GOODBYE AUBURN

The spring was a whirlwind of activity. I was privy to so much coaching information and absorbed as much as possible. We hosted our spring clinic, and Coach Crowe allowed me to do some clinic work in his office on the passing game with high school coaches. A start-up program from Statesboro, Georgia, came in and visited and discussed this way of running the wishbone from two slots all the time—they called it the spread option.

Georgia Southern was born, and a guy named Paul Johnson was on that staff—yes, the future Georgia Tech Head Coach. I had no idea that the future was happening right before my eyes. Pro Timing Day came around, and the NFL scouts were there to test our seniors. Coach Dye brought Bo in and asked the guys to time him if they wouldn't mind. They all gathered forty yards away and set up with their watches. Bo Jackson may have run the fastest time in history at that moment. Every scout started to mumble how they must have missed him and asked Coach Dye to run him again. Coach just smiled and said that would be his only run. The slowest time I can recall was 4.28, with the fastest at

4.17. My word!—he was 6'2 and 228 pounds. I had never seen or have ever seen in my 39 years of coaching a forty run like that. Simply amazing.

We moved into spring practice, and I was actually wearing Auburn gear now and having the time of my life. We did have one problem, though—not enough QBs to run the offense and the scout teams efficiently. The staff decided to use me to throw 7-on-7 drills against the defense during spring practice. I was 23 years old and could still throw it pretty well from working out with our guys, so it was not a problem. However, the drills were set up for 100 percent defensive success. They would give me cards to flash at the scout team for them to learn their routes and then circle where they wanted the ball thrown. I can tell you I got tired of throwing interceptions on purpose. So, I decided to read the coverage and attack the defense. I guess I completed ten or twelve in a row, and Bobby Wallace was losing his mind, screaming at me to throw the damn ball where the card said to. But I just couldn't. They were lighting up these scout team guys, and I have always had a heart for them, so I would just take the ass chewing. Thankfully, though, after practice, Coach Dye came up and told me I had done a helluva job and to keep it up and said he would handle the coaches because I had made the defense better. As I said, he saw everything. Coincidently, a reporter from the Birmingham News was there that day (I believe it was Charles Hollis), and he walked up to us and told Coach Dye the best QB at Auburn that day was me. That was pretty cool, I must say.

This continued daily until time for the spring game. We were in a staff meeting discussing the fact we only had two available QBs for the game and what would happen if one got hurt. No one wanted to put a no-contact jersey on a wishbone QB, and that's when the defensive coaches took their best shot at me. Wayne Hall looked at me and said, "Why don't we put a jersey on smart ass down there and see how he does in full pads?" Oh, crap. I began praying immediately. Surely Coach Dye would not seriously consider this, would he? He remained quiet way too long for my comfort level before saying, "Nah, we ain't doing that. We will just take our chances." I can tell you I sighed a great sigh of relief because I would have played if asked and likely would have been hurt.

The game went off without a hitch, and I got to travel to Destin with the staff for a big golf outing (my second-ever plane ride). I was really enjoying being an official member of the team. That is when Coach Crowe dropped the bomb on me—Jacksonville State had a position open, and he had arranged the job for me. It was a part-time position, and I would have to live in the dorm, but I would be the QB/RB coach making $1,000 a month and have grad school paid for. I thanked him for using his influence to help me, and he told me I needed to meet with Coach Dye and let him know. So, I met with Coach Dye, and he explained why I should stay at Auburn. He said Auburn would win the SEC the next year and that being a part of that would do much more for my career than being at JSU. So, I said, "Yes, sir," and then went and told Coach Crowe of our conversation. Coach Crowe took me outside and had me sit in his vehicle while he verbally assaulted me. He said that he brought me to Auburn, got me my first job, and said I was fundamentally in no position to tell him no. He told me to get my ass back in there and tell Coach Dye I was leaving and thank him for all he had done for me. So, that's what I did. Coach Dye was very gracious and said he understood and wished me well. I spoke with Coach Jim Fuller soon after that and officially accepted the position and became the QB/RB coach at JSU. The 1983 Auburn Tigers won the SEC championship and defeated Michigan in the Sugar Bowl. We went 6-5 at JSU, and Coach Fuller resigned at the end of the season and went to Alabama as an assistant coach. Most of us were fired within a couple of weeks. It is what it is.

I have followed the careers of many of the Auburn staff and players since 1982 but following Coach Dye and Bo Jackson was the most interesting. I saw Coach Dye at a scrimmage during an

Auburn spring practice in 2010. I had not seen him in 20 years, and as I walked up to introduce myself, he said, "Hey Fred, how are you doin'?" As you might imagine, that was a special moment for me. We had a great visit on Pat Dye Field.

Following Bo and his ability to do whatever he put his mind to was as impressive as his God-given raw talents. Equally remarkable was the "Bo Knows" campaign, which resulted from his dealing with a speech impediment by referring to himself in the third person. If I recall correctly, David Housel suggested this to help him with the media. I had hoped to get a chance to run into him again someday. So, 25 years later in 2007, I took my sons J. Michael and John Wesley to Auburn for the Alabama game. Coach Tuberville had invited us to be on the sidelines during warmups. He had met my family while recruiting some of our players at Davidson. The kids noticed Bo Jackson was on the sideline and were so excited, so we worked our way over, and I introduced my boys to Bo. He was very polite and spent a little time with each. I then explained my connection to him from the 1982 season. He thought about it and smiled and said he just didn't remember. I appreciated his honesty. And like I told you from the beginning…
Bo don't know me!

ABOUT THE AUTHOR

Raised in the West Jefferson coal mining country of Alabama, Coach Fred Riley was the first college graduate of his family. He was an All-Conference quarterback and team captain at the University of North Alabama, leading the Lions to their first conference title in 1980. His coaching career has spanned five decades including multiple college and high school stops. Riley's 110-50 record at Davidson High School in Mobile, Alabama, makes him their all-time winningest coach and places him fourth on the all-time Mobile County Public Schools list. Coach Riley and his wife Susan own and operate the Fairhope Storm football franchise, a ministry founded to impact young men and help them become better husbands, fathers and contributors to their respective communities. They are blessed with five wonderful children, three great sons-in-law and three awesome grandchildren (so far!).